CRAZY HORSE

By John R. Milton

DILLON PRESS, INC.
MINNEAPOLIS, MINNESOTA

©1974 by Dillon Press, Inc. All rights reserved

Dillon Press, Inc., 500 South Third Street
Minneapolis, Minnesota 55415

Printed in the United States of America

Library of Congress Cataloging in Publication Data

Milton, John R.
  Crazy Horse.
  (The Story of an American Indian)
  SUMMARY: A biography of the Oglala Sioux who helped defeat Custer at the Battle of the Little Bighorn.
  1. Crazy Horse, Oglala Indian, 1842 (ca.)-1877 — Juvenile literature. [1. Crazy Horse, Oglala Indian, 1842 (ca.)-1877. 2. Dakota Indians — Biography. 3. Indians of North America — Biography]   I. Title.
E99.03M54   970.3 [B]   [92]   74-13056
ISBN 0-87518-063-9

ON THE COVER:
Unidentified Sioux chiefs,
photographed by Edward S. Curtis
in 1905. From the collection of
the Minneapolis Athenaeum.

CRAZY HORSE

Crazy Horse, born around 1842, was a young man when the 1868 treaty at Laramie gave to the Sioux exclusive use of what is now the western half of South Dakota. The discovery of gold in the Black Hills made the treaty no more than a scrap of paper to white prospectors, soldiers, and settlers. Crazy Horse's story is a story of the Sioux way of life, of the Sioux wars, and of the tragic conflict between the nomad Sioux and white settlers.

Crazy Horse was still a young man on June 25, 1876, the day he and his people defeated Custer at the Battle of the Little Big Horn. He died in 1877, bayoneted in a U.S. guardhouse.

Contents

    INTRODUCTION page 1

I   CRAZY HORSE'S PEOPLE page 3

II   CURLY page 11

III   TASHUNCA-UITCO page 19

IV   "GIVE ME EIGHTY MEN" page 24

V   A SEASON OF BLACKNESS page 34

VI   LITTLE BIG HORN page 44

VII   CRAZY HORSE SURRENDERS page 50

    AFTERWORD page 56

Introduction

In the Black Hills of South Dakota, not far north of the town named after Lieutenant Colonel George Armstrong Custer, a man named Korczak Ziolkowski is trying to carve Thunderhead Mountain into the shape of an Indian chief sitting on his horse. By now, the sculptor has removed over two million tons of rock, but it is still difficult to see any kind of shape emerging from the mountain. In fact, it is unlikely that Ziolkowski will live long enough to finish his job, and perhaps his children will not be able to finish it either. But they go on blasting with dynamite, driving in a jeep to the top of the mountain each day, and dreaming of the time when the huge rock sculpture will be finished.

When it is completed, the sculpture will be 641 feet high and 563 feet long, and it will stand as a tribute to the famous Chief Crazy Horse, the Oglala Sioux who helped defeat Custer at the Battle of the Little Big Horn in 1876. As he sits on his Indian pony, Crazy Horse will point over the Black Hills as though he were saying, "My lands are where my dead lie buried."

The Black Hills area was holy land to the Sioux, their *Paha Sapa,* and it was taken from them by the white men who rushed into the Hills after hearing of gold. In fact, it was an expedition led by Colonel Custer himself that announced the presence of gold in 1874. One hundred years later, gold is still being mined in the Black Hills, but Custer is long dead, killed by Crazy Horse's Oglala Sioux. And the white men, who set out to destroy Crazy Horse and all the Sioux after Custer's defeat, are now building a monument to Crazy Horse, who was a great warrior trying to defend his people.

*Sculptor, model, and mountain:
the mountain in the background shows
the rough outline of Crazy Horse's face and arm*

CHAPTER I

Crazy Horse's People

Before the 1700s, the Sioux lived in the area around the western end of Lake Superior in what are now the states of Minnesota and Wisconsin. Their homes were bark-covered houses, but sometimes they used tepees when hunting on the prairies to the west. Usually they hunted in the woods near their homes for deer, bear, and elk, and they fished in the lakes and streams. The Sioux also grew corn and squash, and they ate berries and wild rice. Until the Chippewa Indians invaded their territory, the tribe lived in peace. The Sioux were brave and strong, but they weren't prepared to fight against the Chippewas, who had the advantage of guns that the French had given them.

And so during the 1700s, after fighting with the Chippewas, the Sioux tribes traveled south and west. First they went to what is now southwestern Minnesota, where some of the group decided to remain. The rest moved on to the plains of the Dakotas, Nebraska, and Wyoming. In turn, they had to push other Indian tribes, such as the Omahas, ahead of them. By 1742, these Sioux had horses and were living as nomads, following the buffalo herds on the Great Plains and always seeking new grass for their animals. As they moved, they came into contact with other

Indian tribes — the Arikaras in South Dakota, the Crows in Wyoming and Montana, and the Pawnees in the central plains of Nebraska. The Sioux quickly became excellent warriors on horseback — in fact, they were later called by some military experts the finest cavalry the world has ever seen.

In the middle of the nineteenth century, white settlers began to follow the Oregon Trail westward. By then, the Teton (or Western) Sioux controlled a territory from the Missouri River to the Big Horn Mountains and from the Platte River to the Canadian border. The Tetons were the main group involved in the battles leading up to the Little Big Horn and they are the Sioux referred to in this book. Within the very large area controlled by this group the Sioux were divided into tribal groups. The Oglalas and the Brules lived in the southern part, in what are today South Dakota, Nebraska, and Wyoming. In the north lived the Hunkpapas, Miniconjous, Two Kettles, Sans Arcs, and Blackfeet tribes. In Crazy Horse's time, all these groups together probably numbered between 15,000 and 20,000 people. Compared to the 100,000 white people who traveled the Oregon Trail through Sioux country each year, it is no wonder that the Sioux felt threatened. Not only were hundreds of thousands of strangers coming into their land, but these strangers were also killing the buffalo, using all available firewood, and destroying much of the land they passed through.

Before the wars with the white men began, the battles fought by the Sioux had been small and had not cost either side many lives. Though war brought honors to the Sioux warriors, they could become famous in other ways as well.

5 CRAZY HORSE'S PEOPLE

Finding game, when it was scarce, and bringing it to the tribe, was an important means of gaining respect and honor. In battle, the warriors could become famous without actually killing anyone. Touching the enemy — "counting coup" — was considered one of the bravest feats of all. Instead of remaining at a safe distance from the enemy and shooting at him with a bow and arrow or a rifle, the Sioux warrior rode directly into the battle, up to his enemy, and touched him. This took great courage and skill, and the deed was relived in ceremonies and dances for years afterward. By counting coup, a man could become a warrior and gain fame among his people — as Crazy Horse did.

Most wars were fought among the Indians simply as a matter of survival. The Sioux needed the buffalo, for it supplied them with meat for food, hides for making tepees and clothing and moccasins, and hair and bones for making tools and equipment. The tribe had to follow these herds even if that took them into territories of other tribes. They also needed grass for their horses, so they were always on the move, except in very cold weather.

Since the Sioux were constantly traveling, their homes were now tepees, which were easy to carry and easy to put up. The tepees were made of tanned buffalo skins and were held up by long poles. The bottom ends of the poles were spaced in a circle, and the top ends were tied together in a point. At the top a flap could be opened to let out the smoke from cooking and heating fires. Another flap served as a doorway.

It was the women who set up the tepees and performed all the duties of the camp, leaving the men free to hunt and defend the tribe. They butchered the buffalo, prepared foods to use through the winter, and did all the chores connected with cooking. They also made clothing and moccasins from animal hides. The men considered themselves warriors and hunters. They also kept the only written record of the tribe's activities by drawing the year's events on animal skins, using pictures made up largely of sticklike figures. All other storytelling, singing, praying, and ceremonial rituals were only spoken.

But all was not work and war. The Sioux played many games and often held dances. They enjoyed gambling and the surprise of winning by chance. But they also liked games involving skill, because these allowed them to exhibit some of the skills used during the hunt or during war. They held archery contests, and running and jumping contests. They told old myths, repeating them over and over so that the children would learn them. Music was part of all their ceremonies and dances. Musical instruments were made from natural objects such as reeds, gourds, and sticks of wood. Drums, flutes, rattles, and whistles made a variety of sounds that were strange to the ears of white men.

Before the white men came into the Great Plains, all of the Indian's equipment and tools had to be made from natural materials such as buffalo and deer hide, bone and stone. With the white man came metals, cloth, and glass, which the Sioux quickly learned to use in making their traditional weapons, equipment, clothing, and artwork. Soon they made arrowheads of metal. The white man's guns and ammunition were highly prized, but the Sioux continued to use their bows and arrows for both hunting and fighting.

In their artwork, which was mainly the decoration of

Sioux camp on Ponca Creek

clothing and equipment, only the glass beads were taken from the white man's culture. Paint was made from clay taken directly from the earth. Porcupine quills were colored with natural dyes to make brightly colored necklaces and other ornaments. The paints were applied to tanned deerskins and buffalo hides used as shirts, and to rawhide pieces that would serve as food containers. The geometric designs on all these made them works of art. Later, with the beads provided by white traders, the Sioux became widely known for their beadwork. At first the beads were sewn onto shirts and leggings and moccasins in bright and attractive patterns. Later on, the Sioux made necklaces, bracelets, and headbands. The color patterns and the designs often showed the wearer's religious and ceremonial habits and beliefs, for the colors and patterns represented holy elements in nature. Sioux art was *used,* not displayed in a museum like that of the white men. It was an important part of their personal and community lives.

The Sioux villages, or bands, were tightly knit groups. In some cases it seemed as though everyone in the village was related. Often a person would call his uncles and aunts "father" and "mother." If a man's brother died, he usually married the widow, even if this meant having more than one wife. Family relationships were so strong and honored that if a man wished to show respect for another man he would not only call him friend, he would also call him brother.

Part of this closeness was the result of the Sioux religion, which taught a deep concern for all living things. The Sioux accepted all of life as holy, and all living things as equally important. Man, the two-legged creature, shared the earth with the four-legged ones. Everything that lived was made by the same god and therefore had the same right to life. This is why a Sioux hunter apologized to the buffalo before killing it. Although he had to have the food and hide in order to surive, he still recognized that the buffalo was a fellow creature, as holy as himself, and so he asked the animal's pardon before taking its life.

The Sioux believed in supernatural powers that lived everywhere — in the earth, in the sky, in all directions. And there was one god over all, whom the Sioux called the

Spirit of the World, the Great Spirit, or Grandfather. The voice of the Spirit spoke through many other gods, through the medicine men of the tribes, and through the sacred cottonwood tree, which symbolized life. The Sun Dance and other ceremonies were used to bring forth supernatural forces for the good of the people.

Because of what they saw around them, the Sioux believed that the Power of the World always worked in circles. The world was round, the sun was round, the sky was round, and the nests of birds were round. The sun and moon came and went in a circle. The seasons changed in a pattern similar to a circle. Even a man's life was a circle because he began as a child and when he became very old he was once again like a child. Therefore, the religious symbols and many of the decorations came to be based on circles. The life of the tribe, and of the entire Sioux nation, was seen as a sacred hoop. When the white men defeated the Indians and put them on reservations, the hoop was broken.

Inside the hoop, or the circle, and closely related to the earth, were the four directions. They were like four lines extending from the center of the circle out to the horizon and beyond. Each line represented a different force in a man's life and it was symbolized by a certain color. Black Elk, who was a cousin of Crazy Horse and was also a medicine man, gave one explanation of the four directions. According to him, the West was where the thunder beings lived, the gods who sent rain. Therefore, the West was black. The North was the place of snow and the great cleansing wind, so it was white. The East was the place of light, and there lived the morning star, bringing wisdom to men. It was colored red. And the South was the source of life, or summer, and was colored yellow. When the holy pipe was smoked in ceremonies, it was pointed in all four directions, smoked to the powers of the earth, and then turned up and smoked to the Great Power above all.

All of the symbols used by the Sioux came out of nature. Their lives were tied to the earth, and the sky, and to the living creatures and growing things around them. The hoop of the Sioux nation came from the circles of the earth itself. The cottonwood tree, representing life, was used as the Sun Dance pole. The important colors used in the art were related to the four directions. And even the important numbers came from nature, such as 4 (the four directions), and 28 (the number of days for the moon to become full).

Because of their natural religion, and because they saw that death was an important part of nature, the Sioux had no fear of it. They knew that death eventually came to all things as part of nature's design, and so they accepted it as they accepted all of nature's blessings. This helps to explain why the Sioux were so brave in battle; why they could begin an important fight, such as the Battle of the Little Big Horn, with a shout: "Hoka hey! It is a good day to die!"

CHAPTER II

Curly

At the western end of South Dakota, the Black Hills rise into the air like a sleeping giant stretched out from north to south for seventy-five miles. These hills are the highest point of land between the Atlantic Ocean and the Rocky Mountains. They are like an oasis on the high plains, a place of trees, lakes, and streams in an otherwise dry country. To the west, the plains stretch out as far as the eye can see. To the east, the grassy prairie is like an ocean, with buttes rising like big waves. A day's ride to the southeast brings one into the beautiful but deadly Badlands, with its many-colored rocks that are eroded into deep chasms or rise into the air like great towers. If he wanted, a man could easily lose himself in this hot, dry country that is so unlike the cool, life-giving Black Hills. To the Sioux, the Hills (*Paha Sapa*) were a holy place. Here they gathered to rest and to worship.

To preserve the Black Hills for the Sioux, the U.S. government and the Sioux Indians signed a treaty in 1868 prohibiting white men from entering the area. If this treaty had been obeyed by the whites, there probably would have been no Little Big Horn battle, no Wounded Knee massacre, and Lieutenant Colonel George Armstrong Custer and Chief Crazy Horse would have lived much longer than they did. But since 1833, there had been rumors of gold in the Black Hills, and gold was officially discovered by a member of the Custer expedition in 1874. Soon the rush was on, and the treaty could not keep all the greedy white men out of the Sioux holy land. Gold meant nothing to the Indians, for they saw it as simply a part of the earth. They could not understand the white man's attraction to gold, much less his enormous passion to possess it. But what they did understand was that the treaty had not been kept and their *Paha Sapa* had been violated. It was time for war.

Their war leader was Crazy Horse, who was already widely known and respected because of his courage in earlier battles, and who would later be called the greatest warrior of all. Crazy Horse was determined to punish the white men's injustice and regain the Hills for his people. And he had other ties with the Black Hills, for in the eastern part of the Hills was the place where he had been born.

Some say that a wild horse dashed crazily through the Sioux camp on the night Crazy Horse was born, and that the baby's name came from this coincidence. Actually, his father had the same name, and so did his father's father. Both were medicine men, and their names were greatly respected among the Oglalas.

The night of Crazy Horse's birth, around 1842, the Oglala band was camped on the banks of Rapid Creek. This creek flowed down from the lakes of the higher hills, lakes where melted snow from the winters gathered and began rushing downhill. In the summer, natural springs of water fed the creek. There, one was surrounded by the

*Spearfish Canyon,
in the Black Hills*

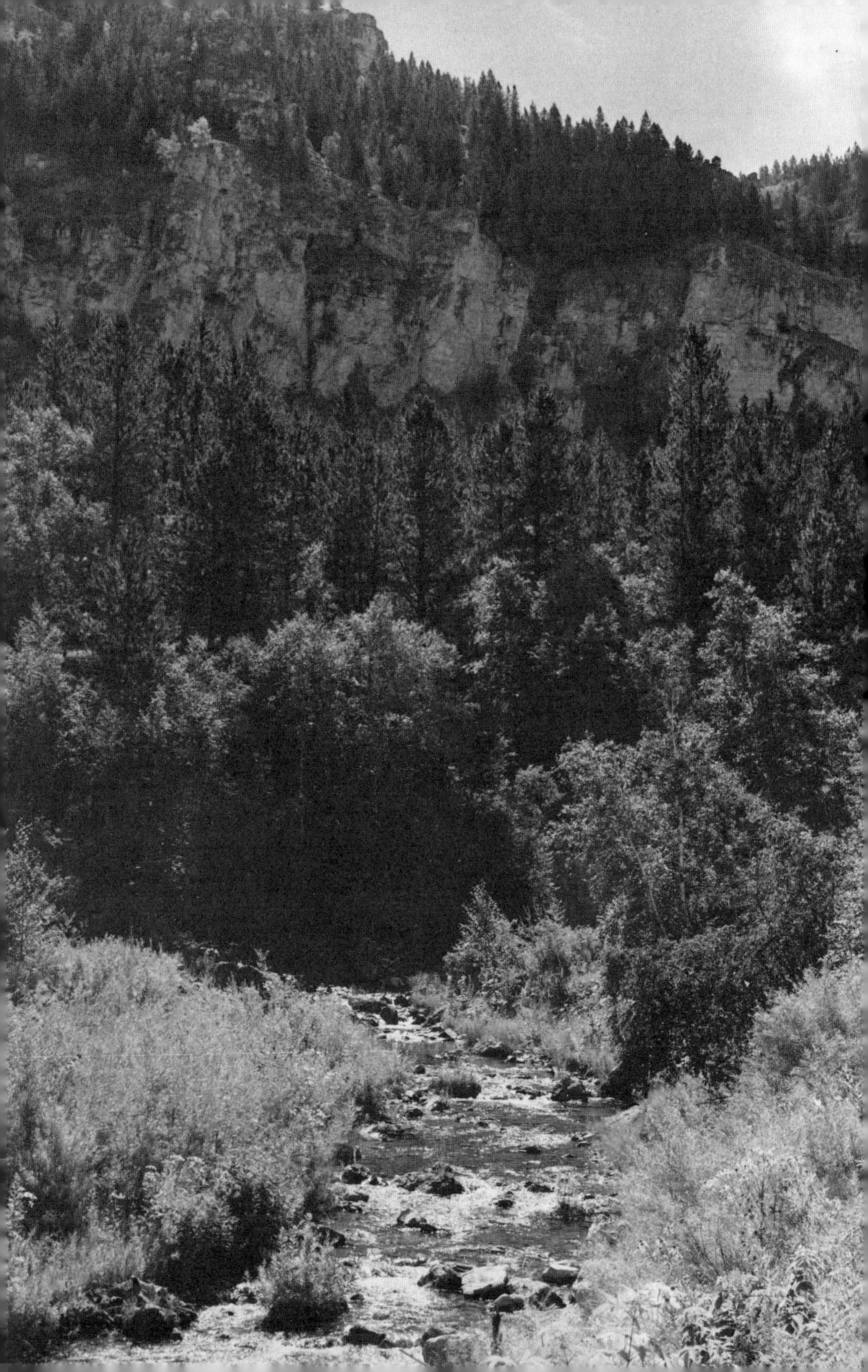

beauties and gifts of nature. When Crazy Horse was born, there was celebrating and rejoicing. A new chief had come into the world.

As a boy, before he earned his family name of Crazy Horse, he was called Curly because his hair was sandy brown and curly, not black and straight like everyone else's. The people wondered at this strange and remarkable boy, and legends began to grow around him. To the Indians, strangeness meant great potential, either as a medicine man or as a chief. Crazy Horse did not disappoint them. When he was still very young, he showed great skill in the buffalo hunts, and a little later he proved his bravery in war. Although he was quiet and stayed by himself much of the time, he had a force and a power that made him a leader early in life.

When Curly was about twelve years old, he had his first vision. It was a Sioux custom for each young boy to go on a Vision Quest, which was expected to bring him to adulthood by showing him the powers that would protect him later in life. For four days, the boy stayed outdoors, usually on a hill or butte, exposed to the weather and changing temperatures, not eating, and often undergoing self-torture. During the four days he had a dream in which he was told how he might receive help from the Great Spirit. Perhaps this would be a song or a totem — an animal or a bird that would always be near him and provide wisdom and good fortune. Almost every young Sioux boy experienced the Vision Quest. But Curly's first vision was not brought about in this way. It was caused by an incident he had witnessed.

Along the Oregon Trail, an old Sioux Chief named

Conquering Bear was accused of stealing a cow from the herd accompanying a wagon train of white men. If Conquering Bear had stolen the cow, it was only because he desperately needed some food. As more and more white men crossed the Great Plains on their way to Oregon or California, they were killing off the buffalo, and the Indians were in danger of losing their food and shelter. But the white men did not understand the Indians' suffering, and the white soldiers shot Conquering Bear.

Curly saw the shooting and watched the old chief die. Greatly affected by the experience, he left his camp and went to the top of the nearby bluffs. Alone and saddened, he went without food and tortured himself in order to stay awake. He looked for a song. All day and all night he stayed on the bluff, trying to make up a song which would relieve him of his deep feelings of sorrow over the death of the old chief. His hunger sickened him, his eyes burned from lack of sleep, and he had to walk on sharp rocks to keep himself awake. But he remained on the bluffs a second day and night, and then a third day. By this time he was very sick and suffering from dizziness. He decided to give up. On the way back to camp he collapsed under a cottonwood tree, burning with fever.

While he lay under the cottonwood tree, Curly saw a man come riding toward him on a yellow-spotted horse. The man was prepared for war and was wearing a smooth round stone behind his ear. Arrows and bullets were fired at the man, but he was unaffected by the arrowheads and lead balls. He continued to ride, now through a storm of lightning, thunder, and black clouds. As though he were one with the storm, he had a jagged lightning streak painted on his cheek and hailstones on other parts of his body. A red-shouldered hawk flew over his head. People surrounded him and reached out to him, shouting. Curly seemed to know what the man was thinking, that he too was sad, perhaps over the loss of the Indian land to the white men. But he felt there was pride mixed in with the chief's sorrow. The pride of a chief whose people were brave and strong.

When Curly woke up, his father and another man were bending over him, shaking him. They were angry with him and thought he had done a stupid thing in going alone to a place where he might have been found by white men or by warring Indians from other tribes.

War with the whites did seem likely. The Sioux had fought several small battles with the white soldiers, and the white men continued to pour into the West. Something had to be done. The Sioux council pipe was sent around to the seven tribes of the Teton Sioux, announcing a peace council to be held at Bear Butte in the northern part of the Black Hills the following summer, in 1857.

Meanwhile, in September of 1856, the Moon of Calves Growing Black, Spotted Tail, who was Curly's uncle and a great Sioux war chief, went with other Indians to Fort Laramie to hear a message that the Great Father (the president) had sent them from Washington. As he listened, Spotted Tail felt the white man's pleas for peace were honorable. Killing had been done on both sides. The wise old leaders were relieved that the white man's army would not punish them for the killings in the past. They were also relieved that the white government would again provide supplies to the Indians.

Curly saw that his people were uneasy, in spite of the

new agreement. The young Sioux wanted to keep on fighting, to punish the whites for all the killing of Indians. But Chief Spotted Tail insisted that it was useless to fight all the white men — there were too many, and the Indians could not win. "Let us keep the peace," he said.

Soon afterward, the Cheyennes clashed with the white soldiers. Several Cheyennes were killed. Curly's father decided to go and help, and he took Curly along with him.

That winter in the Cheyenne camp was peaceful, but summer brought a new unrest and it seemed that war would come. The two leading Cheyenne medicine men, Dark and Ice, promised the people that they would be saved from the whites, but ceremonies must be performed to protect the people against the soldiers' flying bullets. Curly was impressed by the sacred powers and he could feel the presence of the holy ones. As the people joined in the ceremony, he could see them coming together to form a power greater than individuals, a circle of the world. The medicine men dipped their hands in a lake while singing and chanting, then they held their wet hands up in front of them and asked a warrior to aim at them and shoot. The warrior fired his gun at both men at close range, but neither one was hurt. Their magic had protected them from the flying bullets. The people were very happy and went back to camp to celebrate.

After watching all these things, Curly went into the hills to think. The Cheyenne ceremonies had brought the people into a circle, into a tight group, powerful and unafraid. If only he could do the same for the Sioux someday — make them into one body and one heart, strong and courageous. To do such a thing was like tampering with strong fire. It would be a frightening responsibility. But he knew it was necessary.

Curly's planning was interrupted by the news that the Cheyennes had gone on the war path, killing soldiers and settlers. All the people went to the lake and dipped their hands in the water to make them safe from bullets. Then the Cheyennes and the Sioux lined up together and waited for the soldiers, for they were certain that they would be attacked. And soon the soldiers came, many on horseback, many walking behind, and between them were big guns placed in wagons. The soldiers raised their guns and the Indians held their hands out to stop the bullets. They were sure that the bullets would now drop harmlessly to the ground.

But the soldiers fooled them. Instead of firing their guns, they drew swords and attached bayonets to their guns. Then they charged without firing a single shot. The Indians began to run, for they were not prepared for this. Curly ran many miles, and as he ran, he wondered if someone from the Indian camp had told the white soldiers of the protection from bullets. Why else would they have attacked with swords? Almost everyone escaped the soldiers, but behind them they could see their camp burning.

Curly went north in the Black Hills to join the great council of the seven tribes of the Teton Sioux. There he saw the famous chiefs — Sitting Bull, Man Afraid, Red Cloud, Spotted Tail, and others. Looking at the huge gathering, Curly felt strongly that the Sioux were mighty enough to destroy the white men. With a strong leader, one day his people would rise up to take their lands back from the invaders.

CHAPTER III

Tashunca-uitco

The great council at Bear Butte disbanded in the fall and the Oglala and Brule tribes moved west. Crazy Horse and his son Curly rode alone. The boy was fifteen now, and his father knew that soon he must go on the Vision Quest and must receive his lifelong, adult name. Crazy Horse was certain that his son would be a great leader in war and a great medicine man. His own powers would one day weaken, and he must speak to his son before that happened.

On their journey west, Crazy Horse pointed out the valley where Curly had been born. He told his son that these years had not been easy, for the Oglalas had begun drinking the white man's whiskey and had become careless and disorganized. The people quarreled among themselves. They did not have a strong leader to bring them together again. Crazy Horse told his son that a leader must be found from among the young men, someone who was not spoiled by the old troubles.

Curly wished that he could be a big man like his uncle, Spotted Tail, who was a chief of the Brules, or his cousin, Touch the Clouds. He felt ashamed that in this time of trouble he was young and small.

Crazy Horse told him that physical strength would not be enough. The new leader must have wisdom. And, above all, he must have a vision that would enable him to gather all the power of the people together. As his father talked to Curly of the Vision Quest, Curly remembered what he had seen several years before. After his father finished speaking, Curly told him the vision that came to him after the death of Conquering Bear.

I ran from Conquering Bear. His friend was trying to help him, but I knew he would die. I ran into the hills and did not eat. The rocks were sharp under my feet, and I picked one from the ground and cut myself with it. I would not sleep. Nothing happened, and I went to find my horse. Then I was sick and the earth trembled. I did not know if I sat on the horse or had not found him yet. All was a great blur and a great sickness. And then it seemed that I slept.

I saw my horse coming toward me, a man riding him. The trees and sky and grass looked strange, not as I remembered them. And then the horse changed colors, and changed again. It did not seem to touch the ground, and the rider did not seem to touch the horse. His leggings were blue and his shirt was white. He wore one feather, and a small stone behind his ear. He said nothing, but I heard him speak.

As the man rode, darkness came up around him, and arrows and lead balls rained around him, but nothing touched him. People surrounded him and tried to hold him back — his own people, it seemed. But he kept riding. A storm with thunder and lightning appeared above him, and it looked as though a piece

Possibly a photo of Crazy Horse, but he may never have been photographed

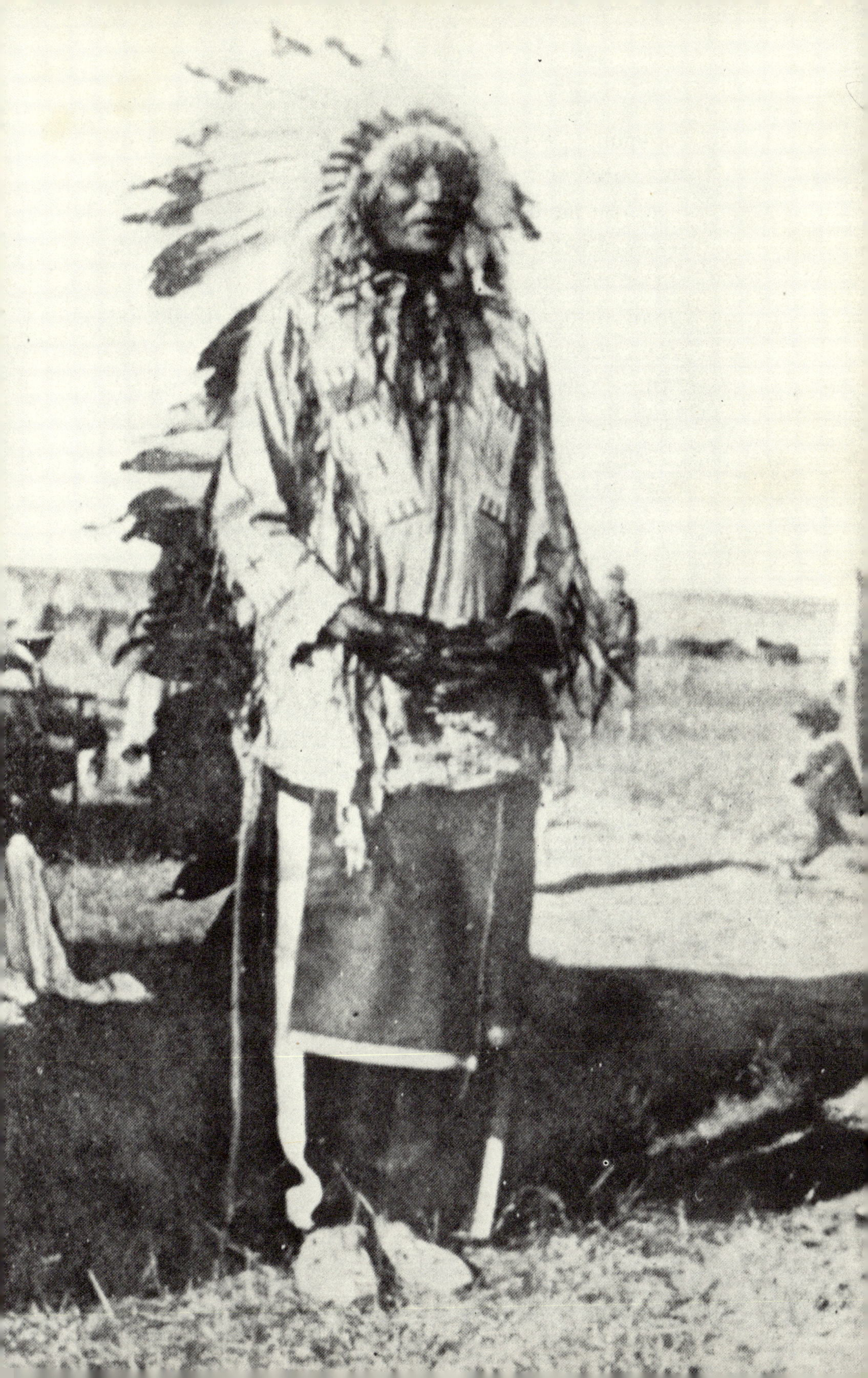

of lightning settled on the man's cheek. Then his body was dressed for war, with only a breechcloth, and spots on his body looked like hail from the storm.

Finally the storm ended, and as he rode the people were close to him, shouting and grabbing at him. Above him, near his head, flew a small red-shouldered hawk, crying out.

After Curly finished talking, Crazy Horse was silent for a long time. Finally he said, "Hau! This is a great vision. You will be the man on the horse."

Yes, Curly knew that. He would be a chief, leading his people into battle. He would dress like the man in his dream, and he would have a hawk with him. If he was true to his vision, he would not be killed by the bullets of the enemy. He would have to be the first in fighting, the leader of his people, even though the way would be stormy and the air filled with lead and arrows and hail. He knew this.

When Crazy Horse and his son returned to the Oglala camp, the band decided to go north into what is now central Wyoming where there were better hunting grounds. After moving north, a war party was formed to go against Crow Indians, who claimed the land, and Curly was ready to go with the warriors. But before the party started out, Curly was accidentally shot in the leg by one of his own band. Some said that the accident illustrated part of Curly's vision — he could not be hurt by enemies, but only by his own people.

A few days after the warriors returned from seeking the Crows, reports came to the village of a band of Indians who spoke a strange language. A group of Oglalas went out to fight them, but the strange Indians had taken a good position on top of a hill and the Oglalas were unable to reach them. During the fight, Curly's horse was wounded and he caught another, a young horse that was difficult to control. Suddenly, the animal was startled by a gun shot and raced up the hill toward the enemy. Curly remembered his vision as he rode through arrows and bullets. He quickly killed one of the enemy with an arrow, and then killed another. In his enthusiasm, he jumped off his horse to take the two scalps, but just as he finished he was hit in the leg by an arrow. He escaped while the enemy fired at him from the rocks above.

Although they had killed only a few of the strange Indians, the Oglalas had not lost any of their own warriors and they had also counted a number of coups. A victory dance was held for them back at the village. One by one, each warrior told of his deeds while the people shouted their approval. Curly was the only warrior to take more than one scalp, but he would not talk about it even when the people insisted.

Curly was only seventeen years old, and his father was very proud of his son's bravery in the battle. Early the next morning, he went into his lodge, put his ceremonial blanket around him, and then walked through the village proclaiming his son a warrior. "I call him Crazy Horse (Tashunca-uitco)."

The name Crazy Horse did not, of course, mean "insane." It meant "enchanted," or "controlled by the spirits." The name had been in the family for many generations, but now it was given to the one who would be the greatest of all and who would be remembered as Crazy Horse when the rest of the family had been forgotten.

CHAPTER IV

"Give Me Eighty Men"

For several years the Oglalas lived happily. They received supplies from the white man's government, but were not bothered by soldiers and dishonest traders and agents. Sometimes they fought with the Crow and Snake tribes and any others that came into their territory. Many coups were counted, and young Crazy Horse continued to perform deeds of bravery and to prove the power of his vision. At age eighteen, Crazy Horse had achieved more honors than most of his fellow warriors would find during a lifetime. Even so, he remained quiet and alone during all the celebrations.

In the village of the Oglalas was a pretty young woman named Black Buffalo Woman, whom Crazy Horse had liked ever since she was born. The two had been very close as they grew up, and Crazy Horse had always somehow felt that she belonged to his own lodge. Now she was tall and lovely and many young men paraded before her, trying to catch her eye. But even though Crazy Horse was very fond of her, he did not court her or try to win her approval by telling his brave deeds in the victory dances. He always stayed on the sidelines, thinking about the things he should do for his people. The Oglalas thought he was a great warrior, but they did not understand his aloneness.

One day a party of warriors, led by Crazy Horse, went against the Crows. Because of the medicine of Crazy Horse, many wanted to go along — Red Cloud, Black Twin, Hump, No Water, several Miniconjous, and Little Hawk, the older brother of Crazy Horse. Before the party reached the Crows, young No Water was stricken by a toothache and asked to return to camp. His battle medicine, which he had seen long ago in his Vision Quest, was two grizzly teeth. He knew that it would be foolish to fight with a toothache, for his medicine would not work. And so he returned to camp. The war party did not get back until two weeks later, after having driven the Crows back to their own country farther west. They returned with scalps and coups to celebrate their victory. But for Crazy Horse there was no rejoicing, for while he had been gone from camp, No Water had married Black Buffalo Woman.

Soon, Crazy Horse was met with more bad news. Rumors came to him that treaties had been broken, new soldiers and a new agent had arrived at Fort Laramie, and with them had come buffalo hunters who carried big guns and killed entire herds. And now many more white men were coming through their country looking for gold, for in 1863 a path called the Bozeman Trail had been laid out through Sioux land as the shortest route to gold country in Montana. The Trail violated the Sioux treaty with the government, but it seemed impossible to keep the greedy whites from trespassing on their land.

In 1864 a large band of Miniconjous and Hunkpapas left the northeastern part of their territory and came into Oglala country in order to stay away from the soldiers in the Upper Missouri. The Indians were gradually being pushed into the center of their land, around the Black Hills. Some time later, they were visiting with the people of a wagon train when a messenger brought news that soldiers had killed some of the Miniconjous and Hunkpapas who were still back at the Missouri River. The Indians then shot some of the people of the wagon train and burned a few of their wagons before returning to the north to help their relatives.

They also took three captives with them — two women and a small girl. The capture of these people troubled Crazy Horse when he heard about it. He did not like taking women as prisoners, and besides, it would mean trouble with the white soldiers again. To prevent an attack by the whites, Crazy Horse and a group of Sioux charged through Fort Laramie and stampeded the soldiers' horse herd. They drove the horses into the hills, and the soldiers were unable to follow. The Oglalas were able to remain at peace for the rest of the year. But then came the news that was to light the fires of war.

In the south, in Colorado, two Cheyenne chiefs, Black Kettle and White Antelope, had been trying to keep peace, but the soldiers would not leave them alone. Finally, the Indian agent found a safe place for them called Sand Creek. The two chiefs and their bands went to Sand Creek willingly, hoping that at last they would be free from the white men. But the soldiers found them there and attacked without warning. The Cheyennes were trapped on the sandy floor of the valley. Colonel J. M. Chivington reported that on November 29, 1864, he had "surprised" one of the strongest villages of the Cheyenne nation, had captured over five hundred animals, and had killed about five hundred Indians including Black Kettle and White Antelope. Chivington was considered by some to be a hero, but many felt he was a disgrace to his uniform. One officer who fought in the attack later wrote:

> We have nearly annihilated Black Kettle's band of Cheyennes. . . . I never saw more bravery displayed by any set of people on the face of the earth than by those Indians. They would charge on a whole company singly, determined to kill someone before being killed themselves. I did not sleep for three days and two nights afterward.

The few Cheyennes who managed to escape the brutal massacre marched north to the Sioux. Crazy Horse was deeply distressed when he heard the news, and he became very angry when he was told of the mutilations performed on men and women after the massacre. The whites must be punished for their treachery.

Less than six weeks later, a thousand Cheyenne and Sioux warriors attacked a stockade near Julesburg, Colorado. Not many soldiers were killed, but the Indians captured pack horses and goods, and burned many houses around the fort. Crazy Horse rode in with the second attack. With him were Spotted Tail, who was no longer talking peace, and Black Kettle, who had not been killed at Sand Creek after all. However, the chief of the Cheyennes still considered himself a peace chief, and after the attack on Julesburg he took his people and returned to the south. (A few years later he was killed in Oklahoma during a surprise attack by Custer's troops. This so-called Battle of Washita was actually a massacre very similar to that at Sand Creek.) The rest of the Indians, including the Sioux and the northern Cheyennes, launched an attack to the north. They killed, scalped, or burned anyone or anything in their way. By this time it would have made no difference to them had they known that Colonel Chivington was being investigated by U.S. officials, or that the famous Indian fighter, Kit Carson, was called in as a witness and said the colonel and his troops were cowards and dogs.

For over a year the Sioux and the northern Cheyennes moved northward in Wyoming with the Black Hills to the east of them. Crazy Horse participated in many raids, and he saw that the warriors were often disorganized, and the young ones were often too reckless and spoiled the plan of attack. Still, he too was young, in his early twenties, and for a time he must continue to take orders from the older chiefs.

In the camps, between fights, the people often talked about Crazy Horse. He was strong in all the fighting, but he never brought scalps to the victory dance or told about his deeds or the coups he had counted. The Oglalas could not understand this. They also wondered why he had not yet married. Crazy Horse still seemed attracted to Black Buffalo Woman, even though she was married to No Water and had a son. The other woman he liked very much was Pretty Valley, a Cheyenne. Why was he interested in a Cheyenne woman? Everything he did seemed strange. Yet, the old ones said, "He is a source of power, and of honor, for our people." Soon, Crazy Horse was chosen by the Oglalas to be the leader of the young warriors and protector of the people in his band.

One of the places where the Indians aimed their attacks

was the Bozeman Trail. Led by Red Cloud, they so effectively bothered the travelers on the Trail that white leaders called a peace council at Fort Laramie. For a while it seemed that peace could be negotiated. The Indians agreed to stop killing the white people who used the Trail, and the whites agreed not to disturb the game, so that the Indians might have plenty of food. But before the talks were finished, Colonel Henry Carrington marched into the fort with many troops and said that he was going to build new forts along the Bozeman Trail to protect whites against Indian raids. The colonel made this announcement at the council.

This was too much for Red Cloud. He accused the white officials of treating the chiefs like children. The Great Father, he said, made offers of peace, sent presents to coax the Indians into giving up the Trail, and then before any treaty could be signed, soldiers came to steal the Trail.

Spotted Tail

Red Cloud

Red Cloud walked out of the council, and about half the chiefs went with him. However, Spotted Tail, who was tired of war, remained and signed a treaty. Carrington then proceeded to build two more forts, one of them called Fort Phil Kearney.

Fort Phil Kearney stood at the eastern foot of the Big Horn Mountains in Wyoming, surrounded by hills and ridges. In the winter, details of men had to go out to gather wood. And it was these men the Sioux went after, because the fort itself was too strong to attack. Up and down the Trail, war parties constantly attacked the woodcutters and the wagons hauling the wood back to the fort.

By 1866 the combined bands of Indians — some thousand lodges — were camped near Fort Phil Kearney. The Indians had decided to destroy the fort and perhaps close the Trail to white soldiers. They planned to lure the soldiers away from the fort, for they were best at fighting on the plains and they did not have the weapons to destroy a heavily protected stockade. This method had worked a number of times; when it failed, it was usually because the young warriors were too impatient and reckless.

Many of the officers in the fort felt that it was foolish to remain penned up while the Sioux went on attacking the woodcutters and wagons. The most outspoken of these officers was Captain William Fetterman. He thought that he could conquer the entire Sioux nation with eighty soldiers, and he loudly boasted about it. "Give me eighty men," he said, "and I will ride through the whole Sioux nation!" But the commander of the fort, Colonel Carrington, had more respect for the fighting ability of the Sioux and tried to convince Captain Fetterman to be cautious.

"GIVE ME EIGHTY MEN"

During the autumn of 1866, and into the winter, the two men argued. Some of the officers began to wonder if Carrington might be weak or cowardly.

The Bozeman Trail ran directly past the fort and up a long hill called Lodge Trail Ridge. One morning, late in December, a party of soldiers went out for wood. As usual, one of Red Cloud's forces attacked them. A signal for help was sent to the fort, and Captain Fetterman felt that this was the chance he had been waiting for. He demanded to be sent out with a relief party. Permission was given, but he was ordered to avoid any unnecessary fighting and to stay on the fort side of Lodge Trail Ridge. Fetterman rode out with eighty-two men in his party, almost exactly the number he had said he needed to whip all the Sioux in the West. It is very likely that he had just that in mind.

As Fetterman approached the woodcutters, the Indians eased off and disappeared into the hills. Meanwhile, unseen by the relief party, a small band of Indians had worked its way very close to the fort. Leading the band was Crazy Horse, with the feathered skin of a red-shouldered hawk in his hair and a streak of lightning painted on his cheek. Most of the Indians walked, but Crazy Horse and a few others were mounted on horses. The horse, the hawk, the lightning streak — these were Crazy Horse's medicine.

He rode slowly along the edge of the brush, the rest of his small band following him. They pretended to hide, but allowed themselves to be seen. This was part of the strategy. Two cannon shots were fired at the Indians and one of them was knocked from his horse. The rest ran away, but not too quickly, going to the north. They shouted as if they were afraid. Crazy Horse himself was the last to go. He appeared to have difficulty controlling his horse, and looked as though he could be caught rather easily if anyone tried to do so.

Fetterman went after him. The woodcutters were already returning to the fort, and Captain Fetterman and his men turned to chase after the small band of Indians trying to escape.

The Indians on foot slipped quickly into the woods, but Crazy Horse and the other mounted warriors kept a fairly slow pace, not getting out of sight of the soldiers but carefully staying just beyond rifle range. At intervals each of the warriors charged back toward the soldiers as if trying to drive them back to the fort. Fetterman thought they were all crazy. He believed that he and his eighty men could outfight any number of Indians. However, he saw only a few, and they angered him. He pushed on, faster, but Crazy Horse stayed ahead of him, leading the soldiers through the hills and up to Lodge Trail Ridge. Here was where Captain Fetterman was supposed to stop. His orders would not let him go farther.

Crazy Horse kept luring the soldiers farther away from the fort. He tried little tricks to make the soldiers think they could catch him. Once he dismounted to have a look at the rope tied around his pony's chest. Later he stopped to check his pony's hoof, perhaps to dig out a stone. And each time the soldiers were encouraged to keep after him, forgetting that they had passed the ridge.

It was the old game of decoy. Crazy Horse, acting as though he could be caught, was really leading the soldiers into an ambush. Behind the ridge, lying in gullies, Red Cloud's warriors waited for the signal to attack. Crazy

Horse led the soldiers over the ridge and down the wagon road to Pano Creek. The trap was ready.

From the throat of Crazy Horse came his war cry. It would not be heard at the fort, and the men back there would not see the attack on the soldiers. It all took place beyond the ridge where Fetterman was to have stopped. The white soldiers were overwhelmed by hundreds of shouting Indians, all yelling their war cries and their whoops of satisfaction. The trap had worked.

The soldiers desperately tried to charge, to retreat, to hold fast in firing lines, but nothing worked. Warriors swarmed in from every direction. Some of them fell before the soldiers' rifle fire, but always more warriors came steadily on. They swung clubs and let loose showers of arrows. Soon only Captain Fetterman and a few of his men were left, and they were on foot. They retreated to the top of a small hillock beside the Bozeman Trail and tried to hide behind a few rocks. It was hopeless. Within two hours after leaving the fort, the captain and his eighty men were all dead, stripped, and scalped.

Before Sand Creek, the Indians had wanted peace. The massacre of their Cheyenne brothers had stirred them to war, and this was their revenge. Now, after the Fetterman massacre, the white men wanted peace. At first, Red Cloud would not give in. Then he demanded that the whites remove all their forts from Sioux country. On these terms, he said, he would stop fighting.

CHAPTER V

A Season of Blackness

In the spring of 1868, many of the northern Indians finally agreed to go to Laramie again for a council. There had been no serious fighting for some time, and they were confident of their power and position. This attitude upset and annoyed the white soldiers, and one of them shot an Indian. Crazy Horse had come to watch the chiefs at council, but when he heard about the Indian's death, he gathered a party, including Little Hawk and Little Big Man, and set out to raid the herds of nearby towns and ranches.

At one ranch, the Horseshoe Ranch, Crazy Horse and his party rode in calling "Hau, kola" (Hello, friend), but the whites barricaded themselves in the station house. Then the Indians set it on fire. The next day they went back, only to find a hole in the ground where the whites had tunneled away. With Little Big Man singing songs about the whites who shoot at people coming to visit them, the Indians followed the trail and eventually found the escapees. They began herding them together like cows. In the short battle that followed, several of the whites were killed, but two showed such bravery that Crazy Horse stopped the fight and sat down with his enemies to compliment them. Later, everyone went back to the ranch where the Indians were given coffee and tobacco and sugar. This ended the hostilities for a while. Clearly, the talk of peace was bigger now than the talk of war.

In the treaty presented at Fort Laramie in the spring of 1868, the Sioux were given the territory lying west of the Missouri River that is now within the state of South Dakota. This land was to be the hunting grounds of the Sioux and all other persons were forbidden to use or occupy it. But what the whites did not let the Indians understand was that this land would be a large reservation, and they would have to live on it at Indian agencies which would supply them with food. The Sioux didn't know they were giving up their right to trade outside the area — at Fort Laramie and at posts on the Platte River.

In May, the southern Oglalas unknowingly signed the treaty and took their presents from the government. Through the summer many other tribal chiefs came to Laramie to sign and to receive their gifts from the white men. But some held out — Red Dog, Sitting Bull, Red Cloud, and others. In the fall, the Tetons met in council and agreed to make Red Cloud their treaty chief. And in November, the Moon of the Falling Leaves, Red Cloud went to Laramie and signed the government's paper of peace. The war was over.

But problems soon arose when the government tried to force the Sioux to move to the agencies. The government also banned trade on the Platte River and any Indians who disobeyed the order were marched off to the agencies. Soon small fights broke out here and there in the Black Hills.

The government, aware of the Indians' unrest, invited

sixteen chiefs to a conference in Washington in 1870. Among them was Red Cloud. Some of the Indians who stayed behind, including Crazy Horse, were not at all sure that the trip was a good thing. After all, Red Cloud had often not wanted to fight the whites, and this reluctance made him appear to be softening toward them. A week or two in the Great Father's city might soften him even more.

Red Cloud was indeed impressed by what he saw in Washington, and he met President Grant twice. He had made the trip so that he could tell the white chief, face to face and as an equal, that white men must not try to control the destiny of the Sioux, that more forts should be abandoned or destroyed, and that the Indians should receive higher payments for their land, especially where the railroads were going through. But he had now seen the power of the white man and he admitted that his people could not beat them in war. Red Cloud pleaded to the white men to be sympathetic and try to undo the wrongs committed against the Indians. Some of the whites in the East did become sympathetic when they heard of the Indians' suffering, and as a result, the Indians received the right to trade at Fort Laramie and on the Platte River.

Red Cloud visited Washington several times in the next years. Although he remained a diplomat who tried to argue for the interests of the Sioux, he saw that the whites could not be defeated and his spirit weakened. He never again led his people in war. The Oglalas looked to Crazy Horse to provide strength and protect them. The new leaders of the Sioux would be the medicine man Sitting Bull and the war chiefs Gall and Crazy Horse.

For Crazy Horse, back in his camp in Dakota, the peace

did not look very promising. Much of the game was gone and the people were hungry. The white man's government did not bring many of the supplies they had promised. Whiskey traders paddled their boats across the rivers every night to sell their bad medicine to the young warriors. It was not a good time for the Sioux.

While the chiefs were still in Washington, Crazy Horse suggested a war party against the Crows. He Dog and many other warriors wanted to go with him, and they all made ready to begin the attack. Before leaving camp, Crazy Horse and his friend, He Dog, received a great honor from the people. The two warriors were made lance-bearers of the Crow-Owners Society and they were entrusted with two lances of the Oglalas. The lances were so old that no one in the camp could remember where they had come from, or when. But they signified strength and power, and caring for them was a high honor.

Crazy Horse led his warriors into the land between the Little Big Horn and the Big Horn rivers, land that was claimed by both the Sioux and the Crows. They came away from the attack with scalps and fine horses. Back at camp, the people said that the real Sioux were still on the plains, and only the peace chiefs had gone to Washington.

Shortly after returning to camp, Crazy Horse went away with Black Buffalo Woman, the wife of No Water. It had taken the warrior a long time to declare his love, and now it got him into trouble. No Water followed the lovers for two days, found them in the lodge of friends, and shot Crazy Horse in the lower part of his face. Crazy Horse fell down as though dead. No Water fled back to camp, told the news, and went into hiding. His wife joined him.

While Crazy Horse was away from camp recovering from his wound, his brother, Little Hawk, was killed by white men as he was returning from the Snake country. Crazy Horse felt that the loss of his brother was punishment for neglecting his duty, and the death filled him with bitterness toward the whites.

When he returned to camp to mourn the loss of his brother, his face swollen and his speech slow because of the injured jaw, no one criticized Crazy Horse, for it was not unusual for a Sioux chief to take a married woman. No Water sent him a gift of two horses as an apology for the shooting, and Crazy Horse insisted that Black Buffalo Woman not be punished.

Soon after, Crazy Horse married a woman of Big Road's band of Oglalas, a quiet but forceful woman just a little younger than his own twenty-eight years. Black Shawl made him happy again, keeping his lodge, saying nothing about Black Buffalo Woman.

But sadness returned to the camp when Crazy Horse's friend Hump was killed in a battle with the Snakes. At first, Crazy Horse was unable to retreive the body from the battleground, but when the Snakes realized that they had killed a friend of the Oglala Strange Man, they left the country. Such was Crazy Horse's reputation.

Late in the summer of 1871, Black Shawl came into the lodge of Crazy Horse carrying a newborn baby girl. She was afraid that Crazy Horse would be disappointed, for every warrior wanted a son who would in his turn become a warrior. But Crazy Horse seemed happy to have a daughter. He named her They Are Afraid of Her, and he predicted that she would be a mother of her people.

About the same time as Crazy Horse was celebrating the birth of his daughter, the white men in Washington made a decision that was to affect the lives of everyone in the Sioux nation as well as the lives of many white men. The last major treaty between the whites and the Sioux had been the 1868 treaty at Laramie which gave to the Sioux exclusive use of what is now the western half of South Dakota. After the settlement in Washington, giving the Sioux the right to trade outside this area, there continued to be small conflicts, but in general, life was fairly peaceful. The Oglalas did more fighting with other Indians west of the Black Hills than they did with white soldiers. Everyone knew that the whites often went back on their word, and might spoil the peace, but very few were aware of the decision that led to war again.

Until now, all treaties had been ratified by the U.S. Senate. Over the years, the other legislators in Washington — those in the House of Representatives — became jealous and angry at being left out of such decisions. As a result, the House acted in 1871 to destroy the entire Indian treaty system. There was also a growing desire on the part of many white people that the Indians should be forced to adjust to the ways of the white man.

Now the U.S. cavalry again began entering Sioux territory on what they called "expeditions of exploration." The motive was pure greed. For years there had been rumors of gold in the Black Hills. The Indians did not care whether there was gold there or not — gold meant nothing to them. But they were violently angry when their 1868 treaty was openly violated by an expedition led by Lieutenant Colonel George Armstrong Custer. Custer came into the Black Hills in 1874 with wagons, soldiers, miners, Indian scouts, and big guns. He reported that there was gold in the Black Hills, and in a short time prospectors from many areas rushed into the Sioux Indians' *Paha Sapa* to pan and mine gold. The federal government tried to buy the land from the Indians, but the Sioux refused to sell. Again Red Cloud wanted to negotiate, and the other chiefs were angered by his willingness to give in to the whites. Red Cloud's powers were diminishing, and the people were now listening more to Gall, Sitting Bull, and Crazy Horse.

Crazy Horse was outraged by this latest breaking of

General Custer and the staff of the 1874 expedition

treaties. The treaty had said that the Sioux would remain in possession of the Black Hills "so long as the grass shall grow." Now the white men swarmed over the Hills digging and destroying in their greed for the shiny metal they called gold.

Crazy Horse led a small party against the Crows, looking for a sign that would show him what to do to fight the whites, but the raid proved nothing. Returning to his camp, he found his people in mourning, the women with their hair cut off or their legs and arms gashed. His father and his uncle came to meet him. "Be strong," they said, and led him to his lodge. Black Shawl sat moaning in sorrow, swaying back and forth. Crazy Horse knew that something had happened to his daughter, and his friends sadly told him she had coughed and choked with a white man's disease and had died a few days before. After only three years of life, she was already placed on her little death scaffold on a nearby prairie. Her rattles and hoops and dolls were hung from the posts.

And so the daughter of Crazy Horse was dead, and the brother, and the old friend Hump. White men were pouring onto Indian land. It was indeed a season of blackness.

Soon the shooting began. Crazy Horse and other leaders took raiding parties into the Hills against the miners, and went beyond the Hills to attack the Crows. It was said that Crazy Horse was becoming more fierce every day, and the enemy feared him because of his magic. His gun hit whatever it was aimed at, but no bullet could reach him. The only thing that kept him from being more successful that first year was a bad winter. The snow lay deep and game was scarce, and the agencies were not distributing food as they were supposed to. There were not enough blankets, and those that were given out were too thin. Finally, the Indians moved next to the soldiers' fort and complained about their agent, hoping the soldiers would provide food when they heard about the Indians' suffering.

Red Cloud and other chiefs went to Washington again, to ask for help. But all they got was another request from the government that they sell the Black Hills to the whites. Nothing was accomplished.

In December, 1875, the Commissioner of Indian Affairs sent a message to all Indian agents west of the Missouri River:

> I am instructed to notify Sitting Bull and all other wild and lawless Sioux Indians, residing without the bounds of their reservation who roam over Western Dakota and Eastern Montana, that unless they shall remove within the bounds of their reservation and remain there, before January 31st, they shall be deemed hostile and treated accordingly by the military.

The agents delivered the word to the Indian chiefs.

At council, the chiefs argued over this order and the white men's desire to buy the Black Hills. One chief agreed to sell the Hills in exchange for six million dollars and rations for seven generations. Spotted Tail suggested a different price. In fact, each chief had different terms which he insisted upon. But Crazy Horse knew all of the arguing was useless, because now the new government was demanding that all of them come to the agency by the middle of winter. If they did not return, then many more soldiers would march into Sioux land.

In March, 1876, an Oglala band was attacked by white

soldiers under the command of General George Crook. It was believed that a man named Grabber, who had been living with the Oglalas, guided the soldiers into the hidden camp. This enraged the Indians so much that they fought fiercely and repulsed the attack. Then they gathered up their belongings and went to the camp of Crazy Horse.

By now, most of the Sioux were convinced that they must unite to fight off the whites. That spring, thousands of Sioux and sympathetic Cheyennes gathered at the Rosebud River. Early in June, most of the people moved west to the Little Big Horn River. But a thousand warriors, including the Oglalas led by Crazy Horse, returned to try and stop General Crook, who was trailing the Sioux people. On June 17, the warriors were attacked by General Crook's army of thirteen hundred soldiers. After a day of fighting, Crook withdrew, for his losses were severe. Crook was baffled by the brilliant leadership and tactics of Crazy Horse.

Later that month, the warriors journeyed together back to the camp at Little Big Horn. Gathered together were between twelve and fifteen thousand people and the great chiefs: Crazy Horse and Big Road of the Oglalas, Sitting Bull and Gall and Crow King of the Hunkpapas, Spotted Eagle of the Sans Arcs, Touch the Clouds of the Miniconjous, Two Moons and Old Bear of the Cheyennes, and even old Inkpaduta representing a few Yanktonais and Santees from east of the Missouri. Now there were between three and four thousand warriors gathered in one place. Here the Indians would defeat the white men in the last glorious victory of the Indian wars.

CHAPTER VI

Little Big Horn

On June 25, 1876, in southeastern Montana, occurred the most monumental battle ever fought between the U.S. government and the Indian nations — the Battle of the Little Big Horn. The battle has fascinated historians for a century, and the story has found its way into hundreds of books, both history and fiction. But the accounts often differ because the fight with Lieutenant Colonel George Armstrong Custer's division of the troops at the Little Big Horn left no survivors among the white soldiers — no one who could tell the rest of the country what really happened.

The Indians who gathered first at the Rosebud River and later at the Little Big Horn were those who had decided that they would be mistreated by the whites no longer. The government was laying the tracks of the Northern Pacific Railroad across Indian lands in Montana. Custer was invading the Black Hills to build a fort for the white soldiers. And now, the Indians had been ordered to a reservation much smaller than the lands guaranteed to them in the Laramie Treaty of 1868. The Indians decided they must stand and try to resist the invading whites.

Crazy Horse was about thirty-four years old at this time.

He and Gall were the main chiefs in battle. As medicine man, Sitting Bull spent most of his time in camp and was not a war chief.

On the morning of June 25, the scene in camp was peaceful. Under the summer sky, wild flowers bloomed along the river, and boys went swimming. The camp was a large one, stretching almost three miles along the river. The people went about their daily tasks. Suddenly there was a call: "Get all women to their lodges! Bring horses into the camp circle! Warriors, prepare to fight!" Scouts had reported seeing more than six hundred soldiers a few hours from camp, and there might be more nearby. (As it turned out, most of the large force, under General Crook, was too far away to help Custer.) Crazy Horse got ready for war, taking off his buckskin shirt and leggings so that he was wearing only a breechcloth, and painting the lightning streak on his face and the hail marks on his body. He thought of the powers of his medicine and also of the medicine of Sitting Bull, who had recently foreseen that a large party of soldiers would attack the camp.

Suddenly, guns were heard from the outer edges of the camp. Crazy Horse armed himself with a bow and arrows, a war club, and a rifle, and he quickly gathered a party of warriors to go with him. The people cheered as they rode out. Crazy Horse took his warriors to the edge of the camp and found that the white soldiers, who were led by a man named Major Marcus Reno, were being overpowered by the Indian warriors.

As Crazy Horse neared the fighting, a white trooper on a panic-stricken horse came riding fast toward the line of Indians. Crazy Horse rode out to meet the runaway and hit the trooper with his club, killing him. Then he rode his horse up and down near the battle line, counting the enemy. He soon realized that they were not many. They had left their horses and were fighting on foot. Why had so few attacked such a large camp? Why had they dismounted when they were so badly outnumbered? Were more soldiers hiding or waiting nearby? The chiefs agreed that there must be more soldiers, and they prepared to meet another possible attack from a different direction.

As more warriors joined the attack on Major Reno's force, he realized that help would not come in time. With as many of his soldiers as were left, he retreated hastily

Major Marcus Reno and his troops

across the river and up the bluffs on the other side. On the bluffs the soldiers were pinned down and held by the Indians' deadly bullets and arrows. Several hours later they were joined by a second force under Captain Frederick Benteen. He too was trapped and couldn't move his men off the bluffs.

Meanwhile, farther up the river, Custer was making *his* attack on the Indians. Custer had divided his forces into three groups. The first two groups were led by Reno and Benteen, and Custer himself led only about two hundred men into the decisive battle against Gall and Crazy Horse. Like Fetterman on the Bozeman Trail, Custer had boasted that he could "take" the Sioux nation with a few men, but he underestimated the number and ability of the Indians and the leadership of Gall and Crazy Horse. In his desire to remain hidden, Custer had not been able to see how many Indians there were in the camp.

Custer's troops were headed north behind the ridges when they were sighted by the scouts. Gall and Crazy Horse immediately set out after the soldiers, leaving behind only enough warriors to keep Reno and Benteen fully occupied and unable to escape. Gall crossed the river below camp to halt Custer before he could reach the river. Crazy Horse rode straight through the camp, gathering up his warriors, and raced north to get ahead of Custer. If the strategy worked, Custer would be caught between the two chiefs.

The battle cry was "Hoka hey. It is a good day to die!" The Sioux were confident that they could beat the bold officer and his famous cavalry regiment. Even some of the boys wanted to take part in the fight. One of them was young Black Elk, a cousin of Crazy Horse's, who was later to become the most famous of the Sioux holy men. It is said that in the first stages of the battle, Black Elk was told by a warrior to take the scalp of a wounded white soldier. Black Elk then killed the soldier and cut off the scalp, his first, and ran back to camp to show his trophy to his mother.

As Crazy Horse raced down the valley (which the Indians called Greasy Grass, and the white men called the Little Big Horn) he saw clearly what the white cavalry planned to do. A small force had been dispatched to one end of the camp in order to draw the warriors in that direction; meanwhile, the larger force would attack the main undefended camp. But Crazy Horse beat the soldiers to the far end of the camp, forded the river, and rode into a ravine which concealed his presence from Custer.

Gall's forces struck Custer first. Then Crazy Horse appeared, and the white soldiers saw that they were being attacked from two sides. They tried to withdraw and regroup. Crazy Horse knew that if he struck hard now, while the soldiers were already in trouble, he should be able to destroy them. One band of warriors was sent further up the ravine to surround the enemy. Then Crazy Horse signaled with his arm and rode straight at the center of Custer's cavalry. He blew his eagle-bone whistle, and his warriors raced after him. Dust rose thick into the air. Although it was early afternoon, the sky was clouded as though night were coming on. Crazy Horse waved his rifle like a flag and then began firing it with one hand, controlling his horse with the other.

As the white soldiers turned to meet Crazy Horse's

charge, Gall hit them again from the other side. Dying horses screamed, and the white men began to run, trying to get away. Crazy Horse did not chase them, but instead, he took his force between the soldiers and their horses, cutting them off from any hope of retreat. When he finished his run through the Seventh Cavalry, the soldiers were disorganized and helpless. But that was not the end. There was to be no escape at all for Custer and his men. The Indians moved in, changing from guns to lances and war clubs, and in a few minutes it was all over. Every white soldier was dead. Lieutenant Colonel Custer, who had boasted of how he could beat the Indians on their own ground, was dead.

On July 6, 1876, the Bismarck (North Dakota) *Tribune* carried a front-page story with the headline MASSACRED. The story read: "Custer and 261 men the victims. No officers or men of 5 companies left to tell the tale." No matter that the Sioux had been attacked by the whites and were only fighting for what had been promised them. They were now "devils" and had to be destroyed at any cost. A great clamor went up to avenge Custer. It did not help the Sioux that their victory was announced just as the United States was celebrating its one hundredth anniversary. The new white nation, destined to become a major world power, was humiliated by "savages" and would not let Custer's death pass by unavenged.

CHAPTER VII

Crazy Horse Surrenders

The great camp broke up after the battle at the Little Big Horn. Crazy Horse took about eight hundred people and started in the direction of the agencies. Perhaps he intended to get supplies, ammunition, and recruits for the fighting that was certain to continue. General Crook followed Crazy Horse with close to two thousand men in his command and fought with him briefly at Slim Buttes (South Dakota) on September 9. Both forces were short of food, and Crook returned to Fort Laramie while Crazy Horse slipped past him to the west and established winter headquarters in the Wolf Mountains of Montana. He was traveling with lodges, women, and children, and he found it difficult to obtain food for the people and for the pony herd.

Even with the Indians' disadvantage, compared to the U.S. soldiers, the military had to devote a large share of its attention to them. By the autumn of 1876, over one-third of the United States' total military forces were concentrated on the northern prairies for the sole purpose of defeating the Sioux. This is a strong indication of the tremendous skill of the Sioux and their leaders.

During that same autumn, a new treaty commission

51 CRAZY HORSE SURRENDERS

negotiated the purchase of the Black Hills. The commissioners went to the various agencies and obtained signatures from a few Indians who wished to stop fighting. Of the great chiefs, only Spotted Tail and Red Cloud were present. The other Indians who were there later claimed that whiskey, bribes, and threats had been used to get them to sign. The commissioners obtained only forty signatures at the Red Cloud Agency, when by previous agreement over two thousand were needed to represent the Sioux nation. In any case, in the fall of 1876 the Black Hills passed to United States ownership.

Crazy Horse may have received word of this latest piece of treachery and it may have made him even more determined to hold out, to remain a free fighting man. His people suffered greatly throughout the winter. It was a cold winter, and Crook pursued the Sioux while they

Officers pursuing Crazy Horse

Officers Torryknee Cantonment, Montana, Jan. 7, 1877, just before starting in pursuit of Crazy Horse and Sitting Bull, and weather 20 degrees below zero. Reading left to right: Lt. Long; Dr. Tilton; Lt. Pope; Brig-Gen. Miles; Lt. Frank Baldwin; Lt. Hayons; Lt. Bailey.

traveled from place to place, hungry, listless, some of them wanting to quit. Even so, Crazy Horse held out for over four months.

In April, Touch the Clouds led one thousand Sioux into the Spotted Tail Agency; and soon after, Dull Knife brought his Cheyennes to the Red Cloud Agency. Crazy Horse continued to hold out for another month, and everyone wondered when he would surrender. Then, on May 5, 1877, he and over eight hundred men, women, and children rode and walked into the Red Cloud Agency. Crazy Horse rode in first, alone. Behind him came ten lesser chiefs. Then came his warriors in a line, and behind them the women and children. The Crazy Horse band made an impressive sight: 146 lodges, about 2,000 ponies, and many guns. The officer who met them came out alone, and he and Crazy Horse dismounted and shook hands. The other chiefs approached and they all smoked the peace pipe.

When this band surrendered, the Sioux War was, for all practical purposes, over. A total of forty-five hundred Indians surrendered at the Red Cloud and Spotted Tail agencies, named after the two chiefs who had been the strongest supporters of peace with the white men. It was these chiefs who helped bring Crazy Horse in. They convinced him that war was hopeless, and that the people who had barely survived the winter would obtain warm lodges and food on the reservation. Even though Spotted Tail and Red Cloud had often been scorned by the fighting Sioux, they were still trusted more than the white men, and Crazy Horse had decided to take their advice. Sitting Bull and his people had fled to Canada, and the Crazy Horse band could not wage war alone.

53 CRAZY HORSE SURRENDERS

During the summer of 1877, while Crazy Horse was on the reservation, he was unhappy and discontented. His life had been spent in freedom, and he was used to hunting and to war and to moving about as he pleased. His restless behavior aroused suspicion, and the military authorities at Fort Robinson (which was near the Red Cloud Agency) thought he was planning something — perhaps an escape, or a new attempt to drive the white men from the country of the Sioux. Crazy Horse insisted that he wished to live in peace, but the soldiers were suspicious, and many other Indian chiefs felt threatened by his tremendous popularity among all the bands at the agency. It looked to many people as though Crazy Horse was still the main leader, the greatest chief, and as though he would try to leave the reservation and organize a new band of fighting Indians.

On July 27, a council was held at the agency with seventy Indian leaders present. General Crook had said that the Indians could go on a month-long buffalo hunt if they promised to return to the agency after the hunt. Young Man Afraid of His Horses suggested that the council feast be held in the camp of Crazy Horse, and at this point Red Cloud and his followers left the council. They felt that the Oglala chief did not seek peace, that he only waited for a chance to escape from the agency and take many of the Indians with him to join Sitting Bull in Canada. The buffalo hunt was canceled.

Other stories were spread concerning Crazy Horse, and finally a cavalry battalion from Fort Robinson (accompanied by No Water, who was unfriendly toward Crazy Horse) rode to his camp to arrest him. Crazy Horse fled to the Spotted Tail Agency and sought refuge with his friend,

Touch the Clouds. Together they started toward Fort Sheridan, but just as they reached the parade grounds Spotted Tail and his Brule warriors arrived to help take Crazy Horse back to Fort Robinson. Crazy Horse agreed to go, on condition that the military authorities would believe him when he said he wanted peace, not war.

But the authorities at Fort Robinson did not believe him — they wanted him imprisoned. Crazy Horse then asked for a council, but was denied the opportunity to have one. Spotted Tail and Red Cloud had gone over to the side of the white man, and so had No Water and many others of the Sioux. Crazy Horse seemed to stand alone, a tragic figure who had done everything he could to uphold the rights of his people, who had fought bravely in a just cause, and who wanted to reassure the white men that he would be peaceful. Later, Crazy Horse would be called by some whites the George Washington of the Sioux, for he was a man who acted for the good of his people. But now, both the whites and many of the Sioux were uniting against him out of fear or jealousy.

On September 5, 1877, Crazy Horse was led to the guardhouse, supposedly to have a council with the commanding officer. But it was only a trick to put him behind bars. When he entered the room and saw the barred windows, he knew instantly what was about to happen. He could not bear the thought of being shut up, and he drew his knife and attempted to run out of the room. Little Big Man tried to stop him and was wounded. Then the soldier on guard duty lunged toward Crazy Horse and thrust his bayonet into the Sioux chief.

As Crazy Horse sank down, it looked as though there

would be an outbreak of violence, and that the Indians who were sympathetic with Crazy Horse would attack the guards and try to get their dying chief away. But the officers reassured the Indians by promising that Crazy Horse would receive medical treatment. Then quickly, they took him away. But it was no use. Shortly before midnight, Crazy Horse died. Touch the Clouds put a blanket over him and pointed to it. "That is the lodge of Crazy Horse," he said. Then he stood up, seven feet tall, and pointed up with his long arm. "The chief has gone above."

Six weeks later, as the government was moving the Indians to a new agency site, eight hundred of Crazy Horse's followers broke away and went north to join Sitting Bull in Canada. It has been said they carried the bones of Crazy Horse with them.

The following year, 1878, the Oglalas, without their chief, were settled on Pine Ridge Agency in southwestern South Dakota, where they are even now.

Afterword

After the death of Crazy Horse, the Indians were relatively quiet until 1890, when a man named Wovoka, who was living in the Southwest, proclaimed himself a messiah and started preaching a message he said came from the other world. Soon, he said, all dead Indians would revive and join their brothers high on a mountaintop. The whites and those who didn't believe would be drowned in a great flood far below. Then the Indians would once again live as they had years before the whites came. But first the Indians must dance the Ghost Dance, for only then would the miracles happen.

The Sioux had spent a miserable winter because of drought, lack of food, and illness. They were ready to believe anything that offered a little hope. The Ghost Dance religion promised a better future, and so the Indians began to dance. The two main centers of the new religion were Sitting Bull's camp at Standing Rock (he had returned from Canada) and Big Foot's camp on the Cheyenne River.

The dancing made the government uneasy about the possibility of an Indian uprising, and the soldiers decided to arrest Sitting Bull. Several Indian policemen, who were working for the soldiers, were sent to get him. A follower of Sitting Bull shot one of the policemen who, as he died, turned and killed Sitting Bull. Now, with Sitting Bull dead, the army turned its attention to Big Foot and pursued him into the Badlands. He was sick with pneumonia and had only one hundred hungry and cold warriors with him, so he asked for a council. But the government said no, he was to surrender unconditionally.

On December 29, 1890, the army prepared to disarm Big Foot and his men, at a place called Wounded Knee. A shot was fired, perhaps by one of the angry Indians, perhaps by a nervous soldier. Instantly, the troops began to fire point-blank at the Indians and into the camp. The Indians fought as best they could with knives and clubs, but when it was all over some three hundred Indians were dead, and about sixty soldiers. The Indian women and children, attempting to run away, were chased by the soldiers and slaughtered. On New Years Day, 1891, a long pit was dug and all the bodies of the massacred Indians were dumped in without any ceremony. It was perhaps the blackest day in the history of the U.S. cavalry.

With Sitting Bull and Big Foot dead, new resistance against the white soldiers was weak and did not last long. By January 16, the Indian wars of the West were over. The Sioux were scattered, most of their land was taken away from them, and they were hungry and sick. What land they had left was theirs only because it was not good enough for any white man. The old way of life for the Indians had come to an end. The sacred hoop was broken.

But the Indians never forgot Wounded Knee. In the spring of 1973, the village of Wounded Knee was occupied by Indian forces under the name of the American Indian Movement, and there was shooting off and on for several months between the Indians and the government forces. Almost one hundred years after the death of Crazy Horse, there still was bitterness between the Indians and the U.S. government, and between those Indians friendly to the whites and those who felt that it was necessary to fight.

Perhaps one day, somewhere in the future, there will be lasting peace. Perhaps then the Crazy Horse monument will stand as a memorial to that peace as well as to the great Indian wars.

Sculptor Korczak Ziolkowski receives an honor from his Indian friends

THE AUTHOR
Dr. John R. Milton is professor of English and editor of the *South Dakota Review* at the University of South Dakota in Vermillion. He is the author of three volumes of poetry and many short stories and critical essays, editor of two books of American Indian writing and art, and president of the Western Literature Association. He is also the author of *Oscar Howe: The Story of an American Indian.*

The photographs are reproduced through the courtesy of the W. H. Over Museum at the University of South Dakota, Smithsonian Institution, South Dakota Department of Economic and Tourism Development, and Western History Collections at the University of Oklahoma Library.

BIOGRAPHIES IN
THIS SERIES ARE

Joseph Brant
Crazy Horse
Geronimo
Chief Joseph
King Philip
Osceola
Powhatan
Red Cloud
Sacajawea
Chief Seattle
Sequoyah
Sitting Bull
Tecumseh
William Warren
William Beltz
Robert Bennett
LaDonna Harris
Oscar Howe
Maria Martinez
Billy Mills
George Morrison
Michael Naranjo
Maria Tallchief
James Thorpe
Pablita Velarde
Annie Wauneka